2000 YEARS

The Christian Faith in Britain

LION
Children's Books

Published by
Lion Publishing plc
Sandy Lane West, Oxford, England
www.lion-publishing.co.uk
ISBN 0 7459 3884 1

First edition 1999
10 9 8 7 6 5 4 3 2 1 0

Typeset in 13.5/16 GaramondITC Light
Printed and bound in Singapore

Text Acknowledgments

5 King Ethelbert's words to Augustine taken from *A History of the English Church and People* by Bede, translated by Leo Shirley-Price, published by Penguin Books Ltd, 1955.
7 Quote from 'The Proslogian' by St Anselm taken from *The English Spirit*, compiled by Paul Handley, Fiona MacMath, Pat Saunders and Robert Van de Weyer, published by Darton, Longman and Todd, 1987.
16 Quotes from the journal of George Fox taken from *The English Spirit*, compiled by Paul Handley, Fiona MacMath, Pat Saunders and Robert Van de Weyer, published by Darton, Longman and Todd, 1987.

Picture acknowledgments
Front cover (clockwise from left)
Celtic cross: Lion Publishing/Ffotograff; Church window: Lion Publishing; Crusaders: Fr 22495 f.43 Battle between Crusaders and Moslems, 14th century from Li Romans de Godefroy de Buillon et de Salehadin, Bibliothèque Nationale, Paris/Bridgeman Art Library, London/New York; Monks: By permission of the Master and Fellows of Sidney Sussex College, Cambridge; Lindisfarne Gospel: By permission of the British Library; Canterbury cathedral: Nicholas Rous; Stained-glass window: Lion Publishing/Ffotograff; St Cuthbert's coffin: University College MS 165, fol. 159, The Master and Fellows of University College, Oxford.
Back cover (clockwise from top)
Stone carving: Lion Publishing/Ffotograff; Norman doorway: Nicholas Rous; Eton choirbook: MS Eton College 178, Reproduced by permission of the Provost and Fellows of Eton College; Parish church: Lion Publishing.
Insides
Title page Snow scene: Lion Publishing
1 Crucifixion by Diego Rodriguez de Silva y Velasquez (1599–1660): Prado, Madrid/Bridgeman Art Library, London/New York; The Sermon on the Mount, 1442 (fresco) by Fra Angelico (Guido di Pietro) (c. 1387–1455): Museo di San Marco dell'Angelico, Florence/Bridgeman Art Library, London/New York; Bethlehem: Lion Publishing.
2 The Book of St Albans: The Board of Trinity College Dublin; Hinton St Mary Mosaic: © The British Museum; Glastonbury abbey: Britain on View/Stockwave.
3 *Candida Casa*: The Whithorn Trust/Dave Pollock; Christian stone crosses: Crown copyright, reproduced by permission of Historic Scotland; Shamrock: Roger Kent; Croagh Patrick: Bord Failte – Irish Tourist Board; St Patrick window: Sonia Halliday Photographs.
4 St Cuthbert: MS. Rawl.D.939, part 2, The Bodleian Library, University of Oxford; Lindisfarne Gospel: By permission of the British Library; Bede writing: University College MS. 165, fol.ii, The Master and Fellows of University College, Oxford; Map: Lion Publishing.
5 Pope Gregory: Keble College MS.49, fol. 61r. By permission of the Warden and Fellows of Keble College; St Gregory and St Augustine: Sonia Halliday Photographs; Bishop's throne: J. Rosenthal; Canterbury cathedral: Nicholas Rous; Whitby abbey: Britain on View/Stockwave; Map: Lion Publishing.
6 St Cuthbert's coffin: University College MS 165, fol. 159, The Master and Fellows of University College, Oxford; Viking model and Viking battle scene: York Archaeological Trust; Alfred Jewel: Ashmolean Museum; Saxon font: Lion Publishing/Ffotograff; King Alfred's translation: MS. Tanner 10, fol. 57v–58r, The Bodleian Library, University of Oxford.
7 William the Conqueror: Dover Publications; Durham cathedral: The Dean and Chapter of Durham; The Bayeux Tapestry (detail) showing Harold I being told of Halley's comet, Musée de la Tapisserie, Bayeux, with special authorization of the City of Bayeux/Bridgeman Art Library, London/New York; Rochester Castle: Britain on View/Stockwave.

8 *Mappa Mundi*: The Dean and Chapter of Hereford cathedral and the Hereford *Mappa Mundi* Trust; Fr 22495 f. 43 Battle between crusaders and Moslems, 14th century from Li Romans de Godefroy de Buillon et de Salehadin, Bibliothèque Nationale, Paris/Bridgeman Art Library, London/New York; Crusader tomb: Lion Publishing/Simon Bull; Murder of Thomas Becket: Keble College MS. 49, fol. 24r, by permission of the Warden and Fellows of Keble College, Oxford; Fr 2810 f. 274 Pilgrims in front of the Church of the Holy Sepulchre of Jerusalem from the 'Book of Marvels' on the travels of Marco Polo from the Livre des Merveilles Bibliothèque Nationale, Paris/Bridgeman Art Library, London/New York.
9 Illuminated letter: Keble College MS. 49, fol. 63r, by permission of the Warden and Fellows of Keble College, Oxford; Chart showing monastic day: Lion Publishing; Plan of Canterbury cathedral: The Masters and Fellows of Trinity College, Cambridge; Illuminated manuscript showing monastic orders: By permission of the Master and Fellows of Sidney Sussex College, Cambridge.
10 John Knox, wood engraving from Theodore Beza's Icones after Adrian Vanson: Scottish National Portrait Gallery; Monk selling pardons: Mary Evans Picture Library; Wycliffe's Bible: MS Hatton 20, 6v–7r, The Bodleian Library, University of Oxford; Portrait of John Wycliffe (c. 1330–84) engraved by James Posselwhite (1798–1884) after a print by G. White, pub. by William Mackenzie (engraving) by English School (19th century), Private Collection/Bridgeman Art Library, London/New York; Martin Luther by Lucas Cranach, the elder (1472–1553) City of Bristol Museum and Art Gallery, Avon/Bridgeman Art Library, London/New York.
11 Portrait of Sir Thomas More (1478–1535), 1527 (panel) by Hans the Younger Holbein (1497/8–1543) Frick Collection, New York/Bridgeman Art Library, London/New York; Portrait of Henry VIII by Hans the Younger Holbein (1497/8–1543), Belvoir castle, Leicestershire/Bridgeman Art Library, London/New York; Great Seal of Elizabeth I: Dover Publications; Queen Mary: Dover Publications; King's College Chapel, Cambridge: Lion Publishing; Portrait of Cardinal Thomas Wolsey (c.1475–1530) (oil on panel) by English School (16th century) National Portrait Gallery, London/Bridgeman Art Library, London/New York.
12 William Tyndale: C23.a.5 New Testament, translated from the Greek by William Tyndale, revised version, pub. Nov 1534 in Antwerp from the Tyndale Bible, (1534): British Library, London/Bridgeman Art Library, London/New York; Greek papyrus: Lion Publishing/John Rylands Library; Tyndale's Bible: Lion Publishing/David Alexander by permission of the British and Foreign Bible Society, London; Chained library: The Dean and Chapter of Hereford cathedral and the Hereford *Mappa Mundi* Trust; Early printing press: St Bride Printing Library/Godfrey New.
13 Eton choirbook: MS Eton College 178, Reproduced by permission of the Provost and Fellows of Eton College; Ornate church interior, wall painting of St Christopher: Lois Rock; Simple church interior: Lion Publishing; Thomas Cranmer (1489–1556) Archbishop of Canterbury, painted after 1547 (panel) by English School (16th century) Lambeth Palace, London/Bridgeman Art Library, London/New York.
14 In Memory of the Gunpowder Treason Plot, 1605 (altarpiece), anonymous, Gaywood Church, Norfolk/Bridgeman Art Library, London/New York; James I: Dover Publications; The Landing of the Pilgrim Fathers, 1620 by George Henry Boughton (1833–1905): Sheffield Galleries and Museums Trust/Bridgeman Art Library, London/New York; *The Mayflower* (model), Science Museum: London/Bridgeman Art Library, London/New York.
15 John Bunyan writing: By permission of the Bunyan Meeting Free Church; George Herbert: Hamish Moyle; John Newton: Mansell/Time Inc, Katz; Christian under Mount Sinai, illustration to *The Pilgrim's Progress* by John Bunyan, pub. by Adam & Son (litho): Private Collection/Bridgeman Art Library, London/New York.
16 Williams Penn's treaty with the Indians, when he founded the province of Pennsylvania, 1661, pub. by Currier & Ives (litho) Yale University Art Gallery, New Haven/Bridgeman Art Library, London/New York; Quaker meeting: Friends Historical Library of Swarthmore College; A Rake's Progress VII: *The Rake in Prison*, 1733 by William Hogarth (1697–1764): Courtesy of the trustees of Sir John Soane's Museum, London/Bridgeman Art Library, London/New York.
17 George Whitefield preaching by John Collett (1725–80): Private Collection/Bridgeman Art Library, London/New York; John Wesley preaching, John Wesley, Charles Wesley: Mary Evans Picture Library.
18 Lord Shaftesbury: Illustrated London News Picture Library; Robert Raikes, children working in a mill, children working in a mine, children at school: Mary Evans Picture Library; William Booth: The Salvation Army.
19 William Wilberforce: Mary Evans Picture Library; Negroes in the Bilge, engraved by Deroi, pub. by Engelmann, c. 1835 (litho) by Johann Moritz Rugendas (1802–58) (after) Stapleton Collection, UK/Bridgeman Art Library, London/New York; Map: Lion Publishing; David Livingstone: Illustrated London News Picture Library; William Carey: Reproduced by kind permission of the Baptist Missionary Society; James Hudson Taylor and family: © OMF International.
20 Christian Aid poster: Christian Aid; Coventry cathedral: Britain on View/Stockwave; Grave, child lighting candles: Lois Rock; Wedding: Olivia Warburton; Nativity scene: Lion Publishing/J. Williams.

Contents

1   2000 Years Ago – the Story Begins

About two thousand years ago, in Bethlehem, a baby boy was born. The boy was called Jesus. His life and teaching changed millions of people's lives all over the world.

As Jesus grew up, teachers, fishermen, tax collectors and many other people came to see that he was unlike anyone else. Jesus taught people about God. He did things that showed people that God was kind and loving. He welcomed people who were unpopular or without friends. He healed the sick and performed many miracles. He told people stories which helped them understand more about God and about how they could follow

Artists over the centuries have painted scenes from Jesus' life. Here, Jesus is shown teaching his followers about God. These followers are known as 'disciples'.

Jesus is born   500 CE   1000 CE   1500 CE   2000 CE

The red bar shows when the events on this spread took place.

God in their lives. Jesus said that people could have a new life if they followed his way and believed in him. Many people came to believe that he was the Son of God.

Jesus had a great number of friends and followers, but he also had powerful enemies. Some of these enemies plotted to kill him. They persuaded the Roman rulers of the country to have Jesus put to death, even though he had done nothing wrong. After an unfair trial, Jesus was nailed to a wooden cross, along with two criminals, and left to die.

A view over Bethlehem, where the Bible says Jesus was born.

But the story of Jesus did not end there. Three days after he died on the cross, Jesus' friends said that they had seen their teacher again. Soon, all Jesus' followers started telling people everywhere about Jesus and about the new life they said God had given him.

Those who followed Jesus became known as Christians because they believed that Jesus was the Christ, or the Messiah. This was the king God had promised, in the writings of the Old Testament in the Bible, to bring people back to God and live with God for ever.

Jesus became important for millions of people through the ages. In this book, you can see how people in Britain have been affected by his life and teaching since the time of his birth.

Jesus died on a cross. Christians believe God raised him from the dead and that God's love is stronger than death. The cross is now a well-known symbol of Christianity.

The Bible

We can read about Jesus in a book called the Bible. The Bible is a collection of writings by different people. Christians believe these people were all inspired by God.

Did you know?

The dates of the Western Calendar are based on the birth of Jesus as a starting point. Dates before his birth are given the letters BC, short for Before Christ. Dates after the birth of Jesus are dated with the letters AD, from the Latin words *anno domini*, meaning 'in the year of the Lord'. Today BCE and CE are also used, meaning (Before) Christian Era or (Before) Common Era.

The First Christians in Britain?

The Romans first arrived in Britain fifty-five years before Jesus was born. They ruled over much of Britain for almost 400 years. The Romans had their own religious traditions and gods, and even thought their own emperor was a god.

Nobody is sure exactly how many Christians there were in Britain at this time. But it is known that there were Christians who were persecuted by the Romans for their beliefs. One of these was the famous martyr St Alban.

Alban was a Roman soldier living in a town called Verulamium probably between 200 and 254. One day he gave shelter to a Christian priest who was escaping persecution. Alban did not know about Jesus and was so impressed when he saw how the priest prayed that he too became a Christian.

The Roman ruler sent soldiers to find the priest but Alban took the priest's cloak from him and put it on. When the soldiers arrived they believed that Alban was the priest and arrested him.

→ A saint is someone who is recognized by other Christians as a holy person, a person who shows God's way. This illustration shows Alban refusing to worship a Roman god. Alban was killed for his Christian beliefs and later made a saint.

Did you know?

? In Roman times many Christians met together in each other's homes. Any group of Christians meeting together is called a 'church'. This word is also used to describe a building in which Christians worship.

Jesus is born   500 CE   1000 CE   1500 CE   2000 CE

The red bar shows when the events on this spread took place.

The judge was furious that the soldiers had caught the wrong man and he ordered Alban to offer sacrifices to the Roman gods. Alban refused because he now believed in the Christian God. The judge then ordered Alban to be beaten. But Alban was brave and still did not change his mind. The judge then commanded that Alban be killed. When the executioner listened to Alban's story, he too became a Christian.

Alban was finally put to death but news about his bravery helped to spread the story of Jesus. The town of Verulamium was later renamed St Albans in his honour.

This is part of a Roman mosaic from the villa of Hinton St Mary in Somerset, which dates back to the early fourth century. It shows a picture of the head of Jesus and, behind his head, the Chi-Rho symbol. Chi and Rho are the two Greek letters that begin the Greek word for Christ – *Christos*. The symbol would tell people that the man was Jesus.

↑ An ancient legend says that one of Jesus' followers called Joseph of Arimathea, carried the the cup that Jesus used during his last meal with his disciples to Glastonbury in England and built a church there. The church burnt down in the twelfth century. These are the ruins of another church built on the same spot as the first one.

3 The First British Missionaries

★ **St Patrick and St Ninian were two of the earliest British missionaries.**

The persecution of Christians by the Romans came to an end after the Roman emperor Constantine himself became a Christian in 312. Then, people were encouraged to become Christians. Helping spread the teaching of Jesus were two missionaries – St Ninian of Scotland and St Patrick of Ireland.

Ninian was born in about 360. He built a church in Whithorn, in Scotland, which was known as *candida casa* – the Latin words meaning 'white house'. From here he travelled around northern Britain and told the Picts, the people living in southern Scotland, about Jesus.

This is what Ninian's church might have looked like. Archaeologists digging in Whithorn have found parts of an ancient building, with cream-coloured plaster still on some of the stones. These could be the remains of the 'white house'.

The story of Patrick is much better known. Some of the details of his life are found in two of his writings which still exist today.

Patrick lived from about 389 to 461. The story goes that when he was only sixteen, he was kidnapped by pirates. He was taken across the sea to Ireland and sold as a slave. For six lonely years Patrick worked as a shepherd.

One night, while he was praying, he heard a voice which told him that his ship was ready. Although Patrick was far from the coast, he realized that he was being told to escape by sea. This he managed to do and he returned home.

Years later, he had a dream in which God told him to go back to Ireland and tell people about Jesus. In 432 he returned. His teaching led many Irish chieftains and kings to become Christians, and he also influenced the growth of

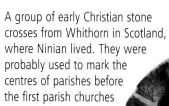

A group of early Christian stone crosses from Whithorn in Scotland, where Ninian lived. They were probably used to mark the centres of parishes before the first parish churches were built.

Jesus is born   500 CE   1000 CE   1500 CE   2000 CE

The red bar shows when the events on this spread took place.

monasteries. Ireland became a great Christian country and a place of learning.

Many Irish Christians followed Patrick's example and became missionaries, leaving Ireland to tell people about Jesus abroad. One such missionary was the Irishman Columba, who founded a monastery on the Scottish island of Iona.

Did you know?

The word bishop means supervisor. A bishop has a special responsibility to lead the church. Sometimes bishops can be seen holding a crozier or shepherd's crook. This reminds people that bishops must be like shepherds and look after those in their care.

There are many stories about how St Patrick taught Christianity. Some say that he used a shamrock leaf to explain the Christian idea of the Trinity — that there is one God made of three parts: Father, Son and Holy Spirit.

A statue of Patrick at Croagh Patrick in Ireland, reminding those who visit of his life and work.

↑ A stained-glass window which shows Patrick with a bishop's crozier. Both Patrick and Ninian were bishops.

4   The Celtic Monasteries

During the Anglo-Saxon invasions, Celtic monasteries helped keep the story of Jesus alive.

St Cuthbert was a holy man who spent much of his life at Lindisfarne. In between periods of time at the monastery, he decided to live on his own on the nearby island of Inner Farne. For many years he prayed and meditated in silence. After his death people called him a saint and admired him for his devotion.

While the Romans were in Britain, they had defended it from invaders. But by 410 Emperor Honorius had removed all the Roman soldiers. Britain was now left to defend itself. It was not strong enough to fight them off and fierce raiders came from Scandinavia and northern Germany. Many Britons fled to Wales, southern Scotland and Cornwall.

The invaders, known as Anglo-Saxons, brought a new language and a different religion. The word 'English' comes from 'Angles' – they were the first English people and modern English is based on the language they spoke.

It was the Celtic monasteries

St Hilda and Caedmon at Whitby

St Hilda was a well-known holy woman in the seventh century. When she was thirty-three years old, she gave up her riches and privileged life in order to become a nun. Eventually she set up a monastery at Whitby, which was open to both men and women. During her time as abbess – as the leader of the monastery – Whitby was a centre of great learning.

Caedmon was a humble herdsman who could not sing or say poems off by heart. Most herdsmen could do this. One night, he had a dream where a man asked him to sing a song about creation. To Caedmon's own surprise, he sang an amazing song. The next day, he went to see Hilda at Whitby. Caedmon sang and everybody agreed he had special talent. Caedmon became a monk at Hilda's monastery and turned many of the stories from the Bible into religious poetry and songs.

Jesus is born   500 CE   1000 CE   1500 CE   2000 CE

The red bar shows when the events on this spread took place.

↑ Here we can see the Bishop of Lindisfarne with an Anglo-Saxon monk called Bede. Bede is famous for writing a history book of the English church and its people in 731. It was the earliest one of its kind and included interesting details and descriptions of daily monastic life.

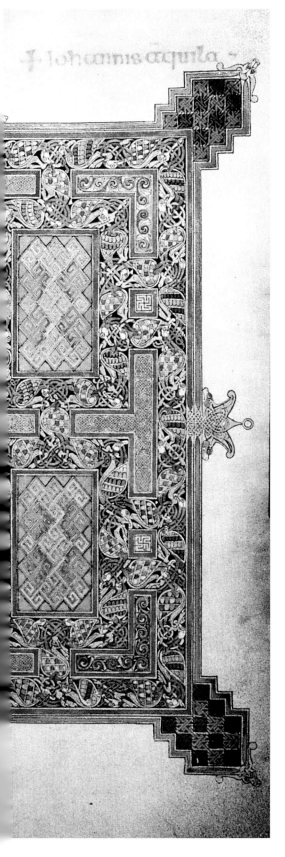

← The Bible was so important that monks would spend many years copying it out and decorating it. This page is part of the beautifully illuminated Lindisfarne Gospels, produced in about 700 and now kept in the British Museum.

that helped to keep the story of Jesus alive in Anglo-Saxon Britain. From Ireland, Brittany in modern France, Scotland, and Wales, the Christian story was passed on by the teaching of holy men and women. In monasteries like St Columba's in Iona (founded in 563), and St Aidan's in Lindisfarne in Northumbria (set up in 635), monks followed a special way of life. They promised not to get married and to live a life of obedience, prayer and work for God. They spent their days in prayer, farming the land, teaching people and reading the Bible – the collection of writings that is central to Christianity.

Monks from Lindisfarne and Iona were active in spreading the teaching of Jesus and setting up new monasteries. Some of the Anglo-Saxon nobles who became Christians went back to northern Europe to pass on this teaching to their own people.

Did you know?

In Wales there are many places beginning with the word 'Llan'. Llan was the Celtic word for church. It is therefore likely that the places whose names contained 'Llan' were the sites of early Celtic churches.

⭐ **Augustine was the first Archbishop of Canterbury.**

'Your words and promises are fair indeed, but they are new and strange to us… But since you have travelled far, and I can see that you are sincere in your desire to instruct us in what you believe to be true and excellent, we will not harm you.'

King Ethelbert's words to Augustine, on his arrival in England (according to the historian Bede).

In the sixth century, the leader of the Christian church, the Pope, was a man named Gregory. There is a story that before he was Pope, he saw some fair-haired children being sold as slaves in the market in Rome. He asked whether they were Christians. He was told they were not; they were Angles from England. He replied, 'Angles… they look like angels!'

As Pope, Gregory did not forget about these Angles. He began a mission to encourage all Anglo-Saxons to become Christians; to 'convert' to Christianity. For this mission, he chose a team of about forty monks to send to England, led by Augustine.

Pope Gregory sent Augustine to England to tell people about Jesus. This picture of them in stained glass is from Norwich cathedral.

Augustine and his men arrived in Kent in 597 where they were warmly welcomed by King Ethelbert, the Saxon King of Kent. Ethelbert's wife, Bertha, was already a Christian and, before long, King Ethelbert also accepted Christianity. Many in his kingdom followed his example. In late 597, the Pope made Augustine archbishop of the church in England – the first Archbishop of Canterbury. King Ethelbert gave Augustine land in Canterbury to build a church, which has remained the centre of English Christianity ever since.

In many ways, then, the mission was very successful for Augustine. But Pope Gregory had also told him to make an

Did you know?

? One church tradition is that every bishop has his own special seat called a bishop's throne. The Latin word for a bishop's throne is cathedra, which gave the name to the churches where the bishop has his seat – a cathedral.

Augustine's throne at Canterbury cathedral.

Jesus is born   500 CE   1000 CE   1500 CE   2000 CE

The red bar shows when the events on this spread took place.

effort at being friends with the Celtic Christians already in Britain. This Augustine had not done. In fact, by taking his own new leadership of the church in England for granted, he had managed to offend many of them. Disagreements over church practices made things more difficult. Celtic Christians and those who followed the Roman ways of St Augustine met at the famous Synod of Whitby in 664 to discuss their differences. Most of the Celtic Christians at the Synod agreed to follow Roman customs.

Iona and Lindisfarne were two centres of Celtic Christianity. Canterbury was the centre of Roman Christianity. It was at Whitby, at the site of the abbey, that leaders of both churches met in 664 to settle disagreements between them.

↑ The ruins of the abbey at Whitby.

← Canterbury cathedral today. Christians have worshipped on this site for over 1400 years.

6 The Vikings and King Alfred

⭐ **King Alfred defended Christianity and his people from fierce Viking attacks.**

The Vikings destroyed the famous monastery at Lindisfarne. Some of the monks saw the Vikings coming across the North Sea from Scandinavia and managed to rescue the coffin of St Cuthbert. They took the coffin to Durham. Many years later Durham cathedral was built to house the remains of this important saint.

At the end of the eighth century, Viking warriors from Scandinavia invaded Britain. This was the first of many separate attacks. Their main aim was to find new wealth and land. They were not Christian but worshipped Norse warrior gods. Christianity in Britain suffered heavily as a result of their fearlessness and ruthlessness.

The Vikings stole valuables and treasures from many monasteries and churches. In 793 they raided the monastery at Lindisfarne and killed the monks who lived there.

They also fought fierce battles against different Anglo-Saxon kings. In 869 they killed Edmund, the King of East Anglia, when he refused to give up his Christian beliefs. Only one kingdom in the whole of England, called Wessex, remained totally independent and Christian, and this was because of its king, Alfred the Great.

Alfred was born in 849. When he was only four he was sent to see the Pope in Rome. Alfred was a remarkable boy for his age and the Pope blessed him.

Alfred became King of Wessex in 871, when he was only twenty-two, and he ruled for

Viking raiders came by boat and settled in many parts of Britain. This life-size model of a Viking boat is from the Jorvik Museum in York.

Anglo-Saxons in battle against Viking raiders. Alfred was the only English king who was really successful in defeating them.

Jesus is born   500 CE   1000 CE   1500 CE   2000 CE

The red bar shows when the events on this spread took place.

The Saxon font at Eyam church in Derbyshire.

A font is used to hold water to baptize people when they become Christians. After Alfred won the battle at Edington against the Vikings, the great Viking leader Guthrum was baptized a Christian.

twenty-eight years. He fought hard to defend his kingdom against the Vikings and finally conquered them at the battle of Edington in 878.

Although Alfred himself could not read until he was an adult, he knew that his kingdom would only do well if his people were educated. He was also determined that England would become a Christian country again. So Alfred gathered together scholars from Wales, France and Ireland to translate Christian books from Latin into Anglo-Saxon. He even did some translations himself. He made sure that his nobles could read and write so that they could help him rule. He had churches built or rebuilt and gave money to help the poor in his kingdom. He made fair laws which were based on the Ten Commandments in the Bible and on Jesus' teaching. Many centuries after his death, he became known as Alfred the Great, the only English king to have that title.

Did you know?

The names of Viking and Saxon gods Tiw, Woden, Thor and Frigg are the origins of the days in the week in English – Tuesday, Wednesday, Thursday and Friday. The Christian festival of Easter takes its name from the Saxon spring goddess Eostre

Part of a history of the English church by the monk Bede, written in Old English. This copy is from the time of King Alfred.

King Alfred only learned to read and write when he was thirty-eight. Later he translated books from Latin into English including a book by Pope Gregory the Great. He sent a copy of this book to every bishop. This is the Alfred Jewel which might have been a marker Alfred sent with the book to a bishop. On the side of the jewel it says 'Alfred ordered me to be made'. Today the Alfred Jewel is in the Ashmolean Museum in Oxford.

7 The Norman Conquest

★ **The Normans built some of Britain's finest castles and cathedrals.**

William the Conqueror wanted to establish his rule firmly. The churches and castles built strongly after the Conquest were a sign of Norman power.

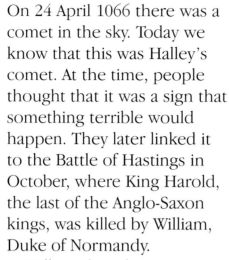

On 24 April 1066 there was a comet in the sky. Today we know that this was Halley's comet. At the time, people thought that it was a sign that something terrible would happen. They later linked it to the Battle of Hastings in October, where King Harold, the last of the Anglo-Saxon kings, was killed by William, Duke of Normandy.

William, later known as William the Conqueror, was crowned King of England in Westminster Abbey on Christmas Day 1066. The Normans from France put their own rulers, lords and churchmen in positions of power. The land which used to be owned by the English nobles was given by William to the Normans. To make sure that they kept their power over the English, the Normans built great castles.

The Normans were Christians and their skill in building was also used to construct huge cathedrals. Some of the finest cathedrals in Britain were built or rebuilt during Norman rule, including those at Durham, Norwich and Winchester. The Normans brought their own trained masons to England and sometimes even used stone from France. Some church leaders thought that building such large and impressive cathedrals would encourage people to be better believers.

Durham cathedral was built by the Normans. Inside are great columns and lofty vaults which give the cathedral a sense of space and grandeur.

Jesus is born   500 CE   1000 CE   1500 CE   2000 CE

The red bar shows when the events on this spread took place.

The Battle of Hastings and the events leading up to it were recorded in the Bayeux tapestry. This incredible embroidery shows seventy-two separate scenes and is seventy metres long. It was sewn in Kent at the order of William's half-brother, Odo, the Bishop of Bayeux. This part shows astrologers telling King Harold about the comet in the sky.

Did you know?

Easter eggs date from Norman times. During Lent, when people remembered how Jesus fasted in the desert, people did not eat meat or eggs. On Good Friday, at the end of Lent, eggs were boiled in coloured water to dye them and then blessed by the priest. They were eaten as part of the feasting on Easter Day.

St Anselm

St Anselm (1033–1109) was abbot of the Norman Abbey of Bec before being made Archbishop of Canterbury by William II in 1093. He is remembered as a great scholar and thinker. He also composed religious poetry. This piece is taken from 'The Proslogian':

Come now, little child.
Turn awhile from your daily work;
hide yourself for a little time from your restless thoughts,
cast away your troublesome cares;
put aside your wearisome distractions.
Give yourself a little leisure to talk with God,
and rest awhile in him.
Enter the secret chamber of your heart,
shutting out everything but God,
and that which may help you in seeking him.

Rochester castle was built by the Normans in about 1130. Its walls are 3.6 metres thick!

8   Crusaders and Pilgrims

In the Middle Ages, many Britons went to places they believed were holy in order to pray and think about their lives.

↑ This map of the world was made in about 1275. In medieval times Christians believed that Jerusalem was the centre of the world and the most important place to visit.

In some churches you can still see tombs of crusaders.

People in the Middle Ages used to travel great distances to visit places they believed were holy. This religious journey was called a pilgrimage and the people who made it were known as pilgrims.

People made pilgrimages for many different reasons: to say thank you to God, to ask God to forgive them, to ask God to heal them. Some people were told by their priests to go on a pilgrimage as a way of saying sorry for something they had done wrong.

For Christians at this time, Jerusalem was the most important place in the world to visit: it was the city where Jesus died and where they believed he rose again. Sadly, Jerusalem became the focus for bitter wars called the crusades.

The crusades were wars fought between Christians and Muslims during the eleventh, twelfth and thirteenth centuries. They mostly took place in countries on the east side of the Mediterranean Sea. Many Britons took part, including Richard I, King of England.

The wars happened for a number of complicated political and religious reasons. In the ninth and tenth centuries, there had been serious Muslim attacks on cities and provinces off the Mediterranean. Western Europeans were worried about losing their power. In 1095 Pope Urban II encouraged Christians to fight Muslims, and in particular to recapture Jerusalem from them. He and the church claimed this war was just, even though Jerusalem was holy to Christians, Muslims and Jews. The Pope told Christian crusaders that if they died in battle, they would go to heaven, and that they could keep any land they captured. As a result, many thousands of ordinary people, knights and barons were fired up with enthusiasm. Many also sincerely believed they were doing the right thing and treated their journey as a pilgrimage. In the earlier wars the Christian

The word 'crusade' comes from the cross which the crusaders had on their clothing and shields. Here Christian crusaders and Muslims are shown fighting each other.

Jesus is born   500 CE   1000 CE   1500 CE   2000 CE

The red bar shows when the events on this spread took place.

crusaders were victorious; in later ones it was the Muslims. The lasting result of the crusades was a deep divide between Muslims and Christians.

The places where Jesus lived were not the only ones Christians wanted to visit. The spot where a saint was buried, or where there were bits of wood, believed to have come from the cross on which Jesus died, all became important religious centres. In Britain, Canterbury, Durham, Glastonbury, Iona and Walsingham were all important places for pilgrims.

Did you know?

During the crusades, special orders of soldier-monks were founded to help pilgrims on their travels. These monks were known as the Knights Templar and the Knights Hospitaller. The modern St John Ambulance Brigade took the name and badge of the Knights Hospitaller of St John.

Jerusalem was an important place for Christians to visit because Jesus died there. This illustration shows Christian pilgrims outside the Church of the Holy Sepulchre in Jerusalem, built on the spot where people believed Jesus had been buried.

This thirteenth-century manuscript shows the murder of Thomas à Becket in 1170 in Canterbury cathedral by soldiers of King Henry II. Two years after Becket's death, he was made a saint. Thousands of people came to Canterbury to see his bones and remember him.

> **Monks and nuns give their lives to worshipping God and serving others.**

Did you know?

The different religious orders were often referred to by the colour of the clothes they wore. The black friars were Dominicans and the grey friars were Franciscans. In towns in Britain today you can often find out where they lived because districts are still known as Blackfriars or Greyfriars.

Julian of Norwich

Julian of Norwich was a holy woman who spent many years of her life praying on her own. She called herself Julian because that was the name of the church next to the tiny room in which she lived.

In 1373 she thought she was dying. As she looked at the cross her priest was holding in front of her, she was sure she saw Jesus. She wrote down her experiences in a book we still have today. In it she describes three things she believed God showed her: that God made the world, that God loves it and that God looks after it.

Monks and nuns were very important to the life of the church in the Middle Ages. When William the Conqueror became King of England, there were only about 1,000 monks and nuns in the country; by 1215 there were about 13,000. These religious communities often provided schools, hospitals, guest houses, help for the poor and farming land for the local people.

Until the late eleventh century, most monks followed the rules set out by St Benedict – they were called Benedictines. Then some monks built abbeys of their own, including one at Fountains in Yorkshire in about 1130. They were called Cistercians. This was a new order. An 'order' was a group of monks following a special way of life. St Francis and St Dominic had their own orders of holy men called friars. Soon, there were lots of different religious orders, each with its own ideas on how best to serve God.

The day in a monastery was organized around eight services: Matins, Lauds, Prime, Terce, Sext, None, Vespers and Compline. Between the services, monks would do manual work, study or write and copy books. Most monastic orders had a routine similar to this one.

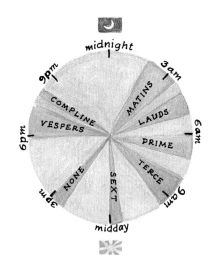

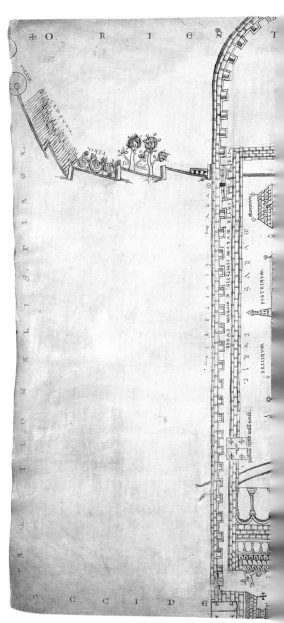

Jesus is born   500 CE   1000 CE   1500 CE   2000 CE

The red bar shows when the events on this spread took place.

The Cistercians had a very simple way of life, giving up many luxuries — even combs and bedspreads! They spent less time at services to make way for prayer, reading and manual work.

St Francis was from a rich Italian family. One day, he went on a pilgrimage to Rome and saw many beggars. He swapped his clothes with one of them and spent the rest of the day begging. This experience changed his view on life — he understood the importance of being poor. Francis said that his followers had to live a simple life and give away all their wealth.

In 1224 the first Franciscan Friars arrived in Britain — holy men who followed his example. They travelled from town to town telling people about Jesus and begging for food and shelter. Today thousands of people still follow the way of St Francis.

Another group of friars were the Dominicans who followed the rule of St Dominic. They believed in the importance of good teaching. Dominicans and Franciscans became well-known teachers in the new universities of Oxford and Cambridge.

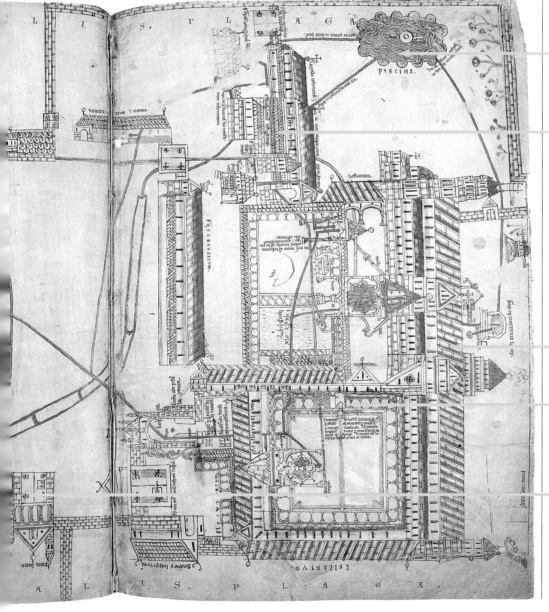

Fish-pond

Infirmary
This was where monks went when they were ill.

Cathedral Church
Services were held here.

Cloisters
This was a courtyard surrounded by a covered walkway, where monks would study.

Guesthouse

← The monastic buildings of Canterbury Cathedral Priory shown on a plan drawn in about 1160.

10 The Rise of the Protestants

By the end of the Middle Ages, the established church in Britain was the Catholic Church; their leader was the Pope in Rome. During the fourteenth and fifteenth centuries, many Christians began to question whether the church was truly following Jesus' teaching. This led to a long period of discussion and argument about how Christians should worship and behave.

In England, a teacher in Oxford, John Wycliffe (1329–84), believed that the church needed change and reform. He thought that church leaders were far too interested in being rich. He said that Christian leaders should live simply and humbly, as the first followers of Jesus had done. Many priests followed his teachings and they were known as 'poor priests' or 'Lollards'. Wycliffe also started work to translate the Bible from Latin into English so that ordinary people could read the Bible for themselves and find out how Jesus wanted them to live. He argued that the Bible had supreme authority, not the Catholic Church.

In Europe, other Christian leaders were criticizing the church too. In Wittenberg, in Germany, Martin Luther (1483–1546) spoke against the way the Pope was asking

John Wycliffe said that all Christians should study the New Testament: 'Cristen men and wymmen, olde and yonge, shulden studie fast in the Newe Testament for it is of ful authorite, and opyn to undirstonding of simple men, as to the poyntis that be moost nedeful to salvacioun.'

Did you know?

In England, many read John Wycliffe's Bible in secret. Each handwritten copy took about ten months and cost £40 to produce. Some of Wycliffe's followers were burnt, with their Bibles around their necks.

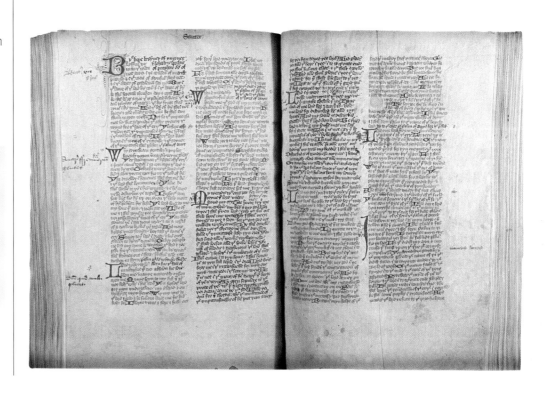

A copy of John Wycliffe's Bible is now in the British Museum.

Jesus is born   500 CE   1000 CE   1500 CE   2000 CE

The red bar shows when the events on this spread took place.

people to buy 'pardons' in order to raise money to build St Peter's Church in Rome. The Pope said that these pardons would guarantee that their sins were forgiven. Luther believed that this was wrong because only God could forgive sins.

These new Christian leaders emphasized the importance of the teaching of the Bible and faith in God over the traditions of the church. Later some of these new leaders formed separate churches. The people who followed these new leaders were known as 'Protestants' because they 'protested' about the existing church and wanted it changed or reformed. Their ideas spread throughout Europe, including Britain. Different groups of Christian churches were called 'denominations'. Europe became very divided: some provinces and countries became largely Protestant; others remained firmly Roman Catholic.

A Dominican friar selling 'pardons' (also called 'indulgences') in a German market square. Martin Luther and other leaders criticized the church for selling pardons. They believed that the Bible taught that it was only through faith in God that people could be pardoned for the wrong things they had done.

Martin Luther was an important Protestant leader. His ideas influenced people all over Europe, and many Christians in England who wanted the church to change its ways. At first, he just intended on reform within the Catholic Church, but he ended up breaking away and forming his own 'Lutheran' Church.

A Scotsman called John Knox (1514–72) worked with the Protestant leader John Calvin in Switzerland. When he returned to Scotland in 1559, he gathered together many of the Scottish reformers. Soon there was a new Protestant Church in Scotland called the Presbyterian Church. By 1560 the Presbyterian Church became the official church in Scotland.

Did you know?

This period in history was later known as the Reformation because it was the time when the people tried to reform the church.

11 The English Reformation

★ **King Henry VIII became head of the church in England.**

Thomas More (1478–1535) was made Lord Chancellor under Henry VIII in 1529 and was an important member of his court. But he was unable to agree with the King over the split with the Pope. He was put to death for refusing to accept Henry as head of the church in England.

Did you know?

? British coins have F.D. written on them next to the Queen's head. This stands for Fidei Defensor, the Latin for 'Defender of the Faith'. This title was given to King Henry VIII by Pope Leo X after the king had written a pamphlet against Luther in 1521 saying that the new Protestant teaching was wrong.

In England it was King Henry VIII (1491–1547) who brought about the great changes in the church. The King wanted a son and heir. He had a daughter, Mary, by his wife Catherine of Aragon, but no son. He really wanted to marry Anne Boleyn who lived in his court but the Pope would not allow Henry to divorce Catherine. The King was so annoyed that he got Parliament, Archbishop Thomas Cranmer (1489–1556), and most of the bishops to agree that the Pope in Rome had no right to interfere in England. He declared that the King of England would be head of the church in England, not the Pope in Rome. By 1534, the Church of England had become separate from the Catholic Church in Rome (this was later known as the Roman Catholic Church). Many people who disagreed with this were put to death.

King Henry divorced Catherine and married Anne Boleyn. They had a daughter who became Elizabeth I. By his third wife Jane Seymour, Henry had the son he wanted, Edward.

When Henry made himself head of the Church of England, he had many rich monasteries closed down. Much of the riches and treasures he kept; some of the money was used to start schools and colleges.

At first, the church in England did not change much. Henry

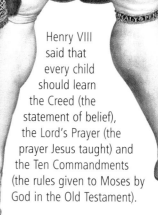

Henry VIII said that every child should learn the Creed (the statement of belief), the Lord's Prayer (the prayer Jesus taught) and the Ten Commandments (the rules given to Moses by God in the Old Testament).

Jesus is born   500 CE   1000 CE   1500 CE   2000 CE

The red bar shows when the events on this spread took place.

Great seal of

himself had been against Luther. But Protestant ideas slowly crept in through his Archbishop of Canterbury, Thomas Cranmer. When Henry died and his son Edward became king, the Church of England broke away even more from the practices of the Roman Catholic Church. Edward died when he was only sixteen. His sister Mary strongly wished England to be Roman Catholic again. Many Protestants were put in prison and some, including Cranmer, were burnt to death. Elizabeth, her sister and the next queen, returned to Protestantism and her first parliament had a Protestant majority. During Elizabeth's reign, the Church of England became the established church.

Queen Mary

A sixteenth-century poet describes the ruined monastery at Walsingham which had been a popular place for pilgrimages before Henry VIII closed it down:

'Owls do shriek where the sweetest hymns
Lately were sung;
Toads and serpents hold their dens
Where the palmers [pilgrims] did throng...
Sin is where Our Lady sat,
Heaven turned is to hell.
Satan sits where Our Lord did sway;
Walsingham, O, farewell.'

The most powerful man in the country after Henry VIII was Thomas Wolsey (1475–1530). He was chief minister from 1514 to 1529, Lord Chancellor, leader of the King's Council, chief judge, Bishop of Lincoln and Archbishop of York. The Pope also made him Cardinal and his special ambassador. But Wolsey did not persuade the Pope to give the King a divorce from Catherine of Aragon. He was charged with high treason and died soon afterwards.

← The magnificent roof of King's College Chapel in Cambridge. The chapel was founded by Henry VI; the windows and screen were added by Henry VIII.

The Bible is the most important book for Christians. Christians believe that the many people who wrote the different books in the Bible were inspired by God.

The Bible contains two main collections of books: the Old Testament and the New Testament. The Old Testament tells of God's work through the Hebrews before Jesus. The Old Testament was originally written in Hebrew. The New Testament contains the Gospels – the stories of Jesus' life, and the history of the early church. These books were originally written in Greek.

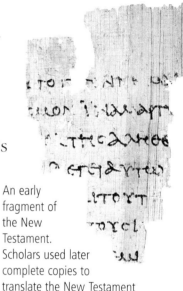

An early fragment of the New Testament. Scholars used later complete copies to translate the New Testament from Greek into English.

In Europe, Latin became the most common written language, so until the fourteenth century nearly all Bibles were written in Latin and copied out by hand in monasteries or other workshops. Bibles were rare and expensive. Ordinary people did not have their own Bible. Although people in Britain had heard the stories about Jesus for centuries it was only when the English Bible was printed that they could read about Jesus for themselves.

WILLIAM TINDALL

William Tyndale, whose translation of the New Testament into English was published in 1526. It became the basis of all English translations of the Bible until this century. Some church leaders did not want ordinary people to read the Bible in English. Tyndale was pursued by secret agents and betrayed by friends. He was put to death in 1535 before he had completed his translation of the Old Testament.

Tyndale's translation of the Bible. This edition of his New Testament dates from 1535.

Jesus is born   500 CE   1000 CE   1500 CE   2000 CE

The red bar shows when the events on this spread took place.

John Wycliffe (1329–84) was one of the first people to put the Bible into English from Latin. Putting a piece of writing into a different language is called 'translating'. In 1526, a scholar called William Tyndale translated the first English New Testament from the original Greek. Copies of the new translation were printed in Germany and sent back to England. In 1538 Henry VIII commanded every church to have an English Bible. In 1563 Parliament said that the Bible and Prayer Book should be translated into Welsh. So in Wales too people began to hear the stories of the Bible and the services in their own language. When James became king, fifty-four scholars started a new Bible translation; in 1611 this became known as the Authorized Version because it was authorized for use by King James I. Since then there have been many more translations of the Bible.

Henry VIII commanded that the Bible in English be put in every parish church. The books were often chained in place as they were so precious. Here we can see a chained library from Hereford cathedral.

In 1476 the William Caxton set up the first printing press in London. These presses meant that books could be set in type and printed again and again. His first books included translations of the lives of the saints.

Did you know?

The Bible has been translated into over 2,167 languages. In English, many different translations have been made over the last five centuries.

13   The Parish Church

⭐ **By the late sixteenth century, services and prayers of the Church of England were in English, not Latin.**

Thomas Cranmer, Archbishop of Canterbury, who made many changes to church services in England.

During Edward VI's reign (1547–53) there were many changes in the ways people worshipped in their local church. Because King Henry VIII had broken free of the pope's authority, the church leaders in England were able to make reforms that they felt were needed. Already, on Henry's order, the Bible was available in English. After Henry's death, Archbishop Thomas Cranmer put together the Book of Common Prayer which more closely followed Protestant thinking. This became the service book used in all parish churches. In the old Latin prayer book there were eight daily services to be said every day by priests. The new prayer book in English set two daily services, matins and evensong, which were for everyone. (There were also other services including those of baptism, marriage and holy communion.) Reading from the Bible was given a more important place in services. Changes were made to Cranmer's Prayer Book over the next few years but most of it survives to this day.

The choir book from the chapel of Eton College is beautifully illuminated. The words are in Latin, and would only have been sung by a choir, many of whom could not understand what they were singing. Gradually church music was written in English so that everyone could understand it.

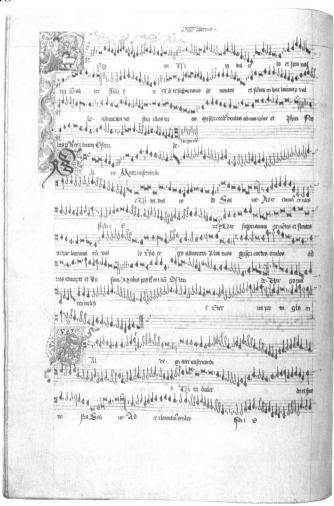

'Lighten our darkness, we beseech thee, O Lord, and by thy great mercy, defend us from all perils and dangers of this night, for the love of thy only Son, our Saviour Jesu Christ.'

Collect (or prayer) for aid against all perils from the service of evensong in the Book of Common Prayer

Jesus is born   500 CE   1000 CE   1500 CE   2000 CE

The red bar shows when the events on this spread took place.

Many parish churches changed in how they looked during the Reformation. Before, the walls and windows of the church were bright with paintings and stained glass. The main part of the church, the nave, was divided from the chancel by a screen. In the chancel the altar was the central focus of the church where the mass or holy communion was performed. The picture on the left shows a church where, to this day, the congregation have chosen to keep to the medieval style.

After the Reformation, many churches looked a lot plainer, like the one above. The interior was stripped of painting and images, and the elaborate screen dividing the nave and the chancel was removed. This remains the style of many churches today.

After the Reformation, this medieval wall painting of St Christopher in a church in Cornwall was covered over to make the church look plainer. It has since been restored.

Now that English was the language of the church there were great changes in the music sung during services. The new prayer book had no hymns in it but often psalms were put into rhyming verse and sung. In 1550 John Merbecke produced his Book of Common Prayer Noted in which music was set to the new services.

In Elizabethan times (1558–1603) people had to go to church every week. The local parish church was the centre of the community. Every church had its priest or vicar and churchwardens. Churchwardens were people who were responsible for making sure that the poor were looked after and that the roads were mended; they also appointed schoolmasters and settled local disputes.

Did you know?

From 1538 onwards all births, marriages and burials were recorded in each parish. From these records people can trace their family trees.

14 Christians Divided

Some groups of Christians did not accept the Church of England's practices.

Today people are able to worship God in the way that they choose, but this has not always been so. During the reigns of Henry VIII, Edward VI, Mary, Elizabeth, and James I there were many changes in the way Christians worshipped. If people did not follow Christianity in the same way as the King or Queen they were often persecuted or killed for their beliefs.

James I

In England, by the time of James I (1566–1625), most people belonged to the Church of England although there were still Roman Catholics and different groups of Protestants.

Roman Catholics in England thought that King James I would allow them to worship as they wanted. But King James made it more difficult for Roman Catholics. In 1604 a group of Roman

Guy Fawkes trying to blow up the Houses of Parliament from the cellar under the House of Lords (see bottom of picture).

Jesus is born   500 CE   1000 CE   1500 CE   2000 CE

The red bar shows when the events on this spread took place.

Catholics which included a man called Guy Fawkes plotted their revenge. They tried to blow up the Houses of Parliament on 5 November 1605 when the King was there. They failed. Since that time, 5 November has been remembered as 'Bonfire Night'.

One group of Protestants became known as 'Baptists'. They believed that people should only be baptized when they could decide for themselves to follow Jesus. The first Baptist Church began in the Netherlands in 1609, spreading to England by 1612 and to America by 1639. Many Baptists became great missionaries.

A painting of the Pilgrim Fathers landing in America in 1620.

The Puritans were a group of Protestants who wanted people to follow the Bible more closely. They believed that Christians should live simply, with no set church services, or bishops or clergy wearing special clothes for services. Many Puritans were put in prison and others sailed to the continent. King James I gave this group of people permission to go to America and start a new life there. In 1620, 102 women and children set sail from Plymouth in a ship called the *Mayflower*. They landed in North America and called their new home New England. This group of early settlers are now known as the 'Pilgrim Fathers'.

Did you know?

The American festival of Thanksgiving dates back to when the Puritans from England settled in America. At first, their crops did not grow well and many people died from disease or poor food. Later they got help from the local Indian tribe who showed them how to grow local food. In 1621, thanks to the Indians, the Puritans had a good harvest. They invited the Indians to join their harvest celebrations. This festival was kept every year and today is known as 'Thanksgiving'.

Did you know?

After 1570 Roman Catholics were persecuted during Elizabeth I's reign. Roman Catholics were not allowed to follow their faith and priests had to say mass in secret. Roman Catholic priests were declared traitors and a special group of priest hunters was formed. In wealthy Roman Catholic homes, priest holes were often built so that the priest could hide if any priest hunters came to the house.

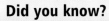

A model of the *Mayflower*, the ship in which the Pilgrim Fathers sailed to America.

15 Stories, Hymns and Poems

★ **Poems, hymns and stories can help Christians remember Jesus' teaching.**

Music, art, storytelling and poetry can all help tell the story of Jesus. In the seventeenth century there were two great writers who came from different Christian traditions but whose writings people still read today: George Herbert and John Bunyan.

George Herbert (1593–1633) was a parish priest, poet and hymn-writer. He was born into an aristocratic family and was well educated. He combined his work as a country parish priest with writing poetry, some of which is now regarded as among the finest in English. Many of his poems have become well known as popular hymns including 'King of glory'; 'The God of love my shepherd is'; 'Teach me, my God and king'; 'Let all the world in every corner sing'.

George Herbert: priest, poet and hymn-writer

John Bunyan (1628–88) also wrote a well-known hymn: 'Who would true valour see'. But he is best known for his story *The Pilgrim's Progress*. Bunyan used to travel around the country working as a metal worker and telling people about Jesus. He belonged to a non-conformist church – a Protestant church which did not conform to, or follow, the teachings of the Church of England. In 1660 Bunyan was imprisoned for his beliefs. He was in jail for twelve years and here he found time to write.

The Pilgrim's Progress is one of the most famous Christian stories ever written. It tells of a pilgrim who sets out on a long journey in search of God's way for him. Along the way, the hero of the book meets many characters. These were often based on

The stained-glass window at the Bunyan Meeting Free Church in Bedford which shows John Bunyan in a cell writing *The Pilgrim's Progress*.

Jesus is born   500 CE   1000 CE   1500 CE   2000 CE

The red bar shows when the events on this spread took place.

people Bunyan knew. The names he gave them told readers about their characters, for instance Lord Hate-Good and Mr Facing-both-ways. *The Pilgrim's Progress* is a great adventure story with a clear message. The hero's faith in Jesus is tested and strengthened as he overcomes the dangers and obstacles put in his way and learns more about God's purpose for his life.

John Newton (1725–1807) was a sailor and slave-trader and a man of bad language and behaviour. When he became a Christian, his life changed completely, and he became determined to use his song-writing talents only to praise God. Among his most famous hymns are 'Amazing grace!' and 'How sweet the name of Jesus sounds'.

A nineteenth-century painting of a scene from *The Pilgrim's Progress* by John Bunyan, showing the main character Christian under Mount

Amazing grace!

Amazing grace! How sweet the sound
That saved a wretch like me;
I once was lost, but now am found,
Was blind but now can see.

'Twas grace that taught my heart to fear,
And grace my fears relieved;
How precious did that grace appear,
The hour I first believed!

Through many dangers, toils and snares
I have already come:
'Tis grace that brought me safe thus far,
And grace will lead me home.

16 George Fox and the Quakers

⭐ **Quakers believed that faith led people to do good work.**

George Fox travelled throughout Britain and across the Atlantic ocean to Barbados and Jamaica and to the American colonies. For these long journeys he made his coat and breeches of leather because they were hardwearing. He was a famous speaker and when people heard that the man in leather breeches was coming they used to go out and see him.

'My desires after the Lord grew stronger, and zeal in the pure knowledge of God and of Christ alone, without the help of any man, book or writing. For though I read the Scriptures that spoke of Christ and of God, yet I knew him not but by revelation, as he who hath the key did open, and as the Father of life drew me to his Son by his Spirit.'

From the journal of George Fox

In 1682 William Penn (1644–1718) set sail for America with a group of Friends to start a colony of Friends where they could live in the way they chose. They settled in Pennsylvania, named after Penn's father, and called their capital Philadelphia, which means 'brotherly love'.

Throughout Christian history in Britain there have been men and women who have shown people more about God by their life and actions. One group of Christians who became noted for their tireless enthusiasm to do good was inspired by a man named George Fox (1624–91). George Fox was an apprentice to a shoemaker. When he was twenty-three, he had a religious experience which changed his life. In his journal, he wrote, 'And when all my hopes in all men were gone, so that I had nothing outwardly to help me, nor could tell what to do, then Oh then, I heard a voice which said, "There is one, even Christ Jesus, that can speak to thy condition," and when I heard it, my heart did leap for joy.'

George Fox went around the country telling people that they needed to find the inner voice of God. He believed that God did not live in temples and churches made by human hands but in people's hearts. George Fox also said that this direct experience of God led people to do good.

Many people followed George Fox. They used to meet together and instead of following a traditional church service they used to sit in silence until they felt that God was leading them to say something or pray. Other Christians made fun of them and said that Fox's followers used to tremble and quake with emotion as they waited upon God. They called the new group 'Quakers'.

Jesus is born   500 CE   1000 CE   1500 CE   2000 CE
| | | | |

The red bar shows when the events on this spread took place.

Another name for them was the 'Friends' because they believed that if people had the right relationship with God they were friends with each other.

The Friends have always believed that their faith leads them to put right the things in the world around them that are wrong. They also believe that it is wrong to fight. So over the centuries Friends and Quakers have worked to help those in distress and improve unfair conditions in society.

A drawing of a Quaker meeting house. The congregation are seated so that they can talk and listen to each other, instead of in rows all facing in the same direction.

Elizabeth Fry (1780–1845) was a Friend who worked for many years to improve the conditions in Britain's prisons. In those days prisons were full of men, women and children, as shown in this painting by William Hogarth. Elizabeth Fry set up a school for the children and workshops for the women in Newgate prison in London.

17 Methodism and the Wesley Brothers

⭐ **The Wesley brothers travelled all over the country to tell people the story of Jesus.**

George Whitefield came to know the Wesley brothers at Oxford. He travelled all over Britain and America telling people about Jesus. Huge crowds came to listen to him wherever he went. He had to preach in the open air as the churches could not hold everyone. John Wesley followed Whitefield's example of preaching in the open.

John Wesley (1703–91) and Charles Wesley (1707–88) are the most famous brothers in the history of Christianity in Britain. John and Charles were two of nineteen children born to Susannah and Samuel Wesley. Samuel Wesley was a Church of England vicar in Epworth in Lincolnshire. The two brothers went to the University of Oxford and were serious students. John Wesley kept a detailed account of all his activities throughout the day and told his friends to do the same and be 'methodical' so that they could make sure that all their time was put to God's work. Some say this is why they were called Methodists – which later became the name of their many followers.

The brothers began their work as missionaries by travelling to Georgia in America to tell people about Jesus. John and Charles

Jesus is born   500 CE   1000 CE   1500 CE   2000 CE

The red bar shows when the events on this spread took place.

believed in the importance of people having a direct experience of God. John Wesley described this experience as 'I felt my heart strangely warmed'. The Wesley brothers went on long tours around Britain, riding on horseback and stopping at different towns and villages to pass on the Christian story to all who would listen.

Like the Quakers, Methodists emphasized the importance of helping people. They set up dispensaries, schools, old people's homes and orphanages.

John Wesley

Charles Wesley is regarded as one of the greatest of all hymn-writers. He used these religious songs to help teach others the Christian faith. He is thought to have written about 6000 hymns including 'Hark! the herald angels sing', 'Love divine all loves excelling' and 'Hail the day that sees him rise'.

Charles Wesley

Did you know?

When he was only five, John Wesley was rescued from a fire at his home a few minutes before the roof fell in. His mother was convinced that God had saved him for some special purpose.

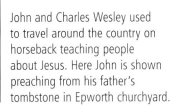

John and Charles Wesley used to travel around the country on horseback teaching people about Jesus. Here John is shown preaching from his father's tombstone in Epworth churchyard.

★ **Until the nineteenth century, most children in Britain did not go to school. Education for poor children was first provided by churches.**

Lord Shaftesbury was very aware of the struggles of poor people to make a living and the dreadful conditions in which children worked. Even though he was a member of the aristocracy, he was prepared to go down coal mines and work as a London barrow boy to experience the conditions for himself. He entered Parliament and succeeded in changing the law on child labour.

The title page of a book published in 1853 about the ill-treatment of children in English factories. Children worked long hours in dangerous conditions. In the cotton mills they used to have to sweep under the unguarded machines while they were still moving.

In the eighteenth and nineteenth centuries, lifestyles in Britain changed dramatically as more and more people were needed to work in the new industries. Conditions of work were often terrible. Christians took the lead in working to improve things. Providing schooling for children was one way of protecting children from bad working conditions and helping them to a better future.

In 1811 a group of people in London formed 'The National Society' for setting up church day schools to provide free education for the poor and to teach Christianity. These were Church of England schools. Other churches soon followed their example. It was only in 1870 that the British Government decided that the government should provide education for all children and by 1880 every child aged between the ages of five and ten had to go to school. To this day many primary and secondary schools are church schools.

In 1780 Robert Raikes opened the first Sunday school. For many children Sunday schools were the only chance they had to learn to read and write and hear about Christianity. These Sunday schools became popular and many towns followed Raikes' example.

THE
WHITE SLAVES
OF
ENGLAND.

Some children were forced to work in the coal mines under terrible conditions. Here boys drag a trolley full of coal along an underground passage which is so low that they are unable to stand up.

Jesus is born   500 CE   1000 CE   1500 CE   2000 CE

The red bar shows when the events on this spread took place.

Many Christian leaders in Britain in the nineteenth century worked to change unjust laws. Millions of children had to work long hours in horrible conditions in mines, factories and fields. Charles Kingsley (1819–75), a vicar in Hampshire, wrote stories and poems about these child workers. His most famous, *The Water Babies*, helped show people how cruel life could be for children.

Another leader, the Earl of Shaftesbury (1801–85), believed that it was his duty to God to help the poor. He entered Parliament and worked to improve the working conditions in factories and coal mines. Eventually laws were passed to stop child labour.

William Booth (1829–1912) was a Methodist who was shocked by the great poverty in the East End of London. He set up the Salvation Army, a Christian organization which, through its music and its preaching, took the Christian message onto the streets of London. The Salvation Army has always combined telling the gospel story with active social work.

Afternoon assembly at a school in London

19 The Missionary Movement

★ **In the nineteenth century, the Christian story was taken by missionaries around the world.**

William Wilberforce (1759–1833) was a Christian who believed that he had to change the injustices in society. 'There was needed some reformer of the nation's morals and who should raise his voice in the high places of the land.' He is best remembered for his work towards the abolition of slavery. He campaigned against the terrible conditions slaves suffered in ships from Africa to America and the West Indies, and their sufferings on the plantations. In 1833, three days before he died, a law was passed to end slavery in all parts of the British Empire.

By 1899 the British had made one fifth of the world their empire. In the two centuries before that time, there were many British Christian missionaries who travelled to countries that the British were exploring and adding to their empire, to tell people about Jesus.

William Carey (1761–1834), believed that it was every Christian's job to preach the gospel throughout the world. Carey was a shoemaker from Northamptonshire who sailed to Bengal in 1793. He translated the Bible into Bengali so that the local people could hear about Jesus in their own language. Missionaries not only told people about Jesus but they also set up schools and hospitals. They tried to show Jesus' love through their words and actions. Today Christianity is growing in many of the countries the first missionaries went to and missionaries from Asia, Latin America and Africa come to Britain to encourage Christians here.

Africans were taken from their homes and transported across the Atlantic Ocean to work on the plantations of America. During the voyage they were kept chained together in the overcrowded bilge of the ship. Ill-treatment, disease and insufficient food meant that many did not survive the journey.

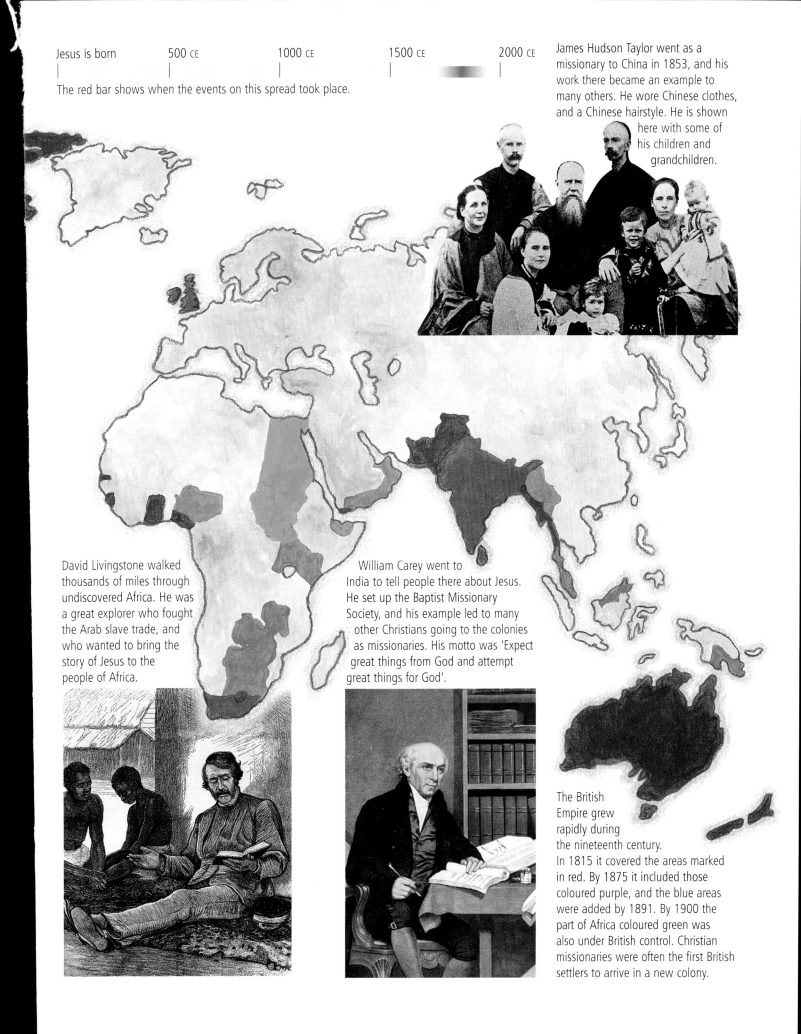

Jesus is born | 500 CE | 1000 CE | 1500 CE | 2000 CE

The red bar shows when the events on this spread took place.

James Hudson Taylor went as a missionary to China in 1853, and his work there became an example to many others. He wore Chinese clothes, and a Chinese hairstyle. He is shown here with some of his children and grandchildren.

David Livingstone walked thousands of miles through undiscovered Africa. He was a great explorer who fought the Arab slave trade, and who wanted to bring the story of Jesus to the people of Africa.

William Carey went to India to tell people there about Jesus. He set up the Baptist Missionary Society, and his example led to many other Christians going to the colonies as missionaries. His motto was 'Expect great things from God and attempt great things for God'.

The British Empire grew rapidly during the nineteenth century. In 1815 it covered the areas marked in red. By 1875 it included those coloured purple, and the blue areas were added by 1891. By 1900 the part of Africa coloured green was also under British control. Christian missionaries were often the first British settlers to arrive in a new colony.

Christian traditions continue to play a part in a multi-faith society.

By the beginning of the twentieth century, the landscape of Britain clearly showed its long Christian heritage. In every village and town in the country, there were signs of Christianity in the churches, chapels and crosses, and the names of schools, buildings and streets. For many people at this time, Sunday meant going to church, and a large number of community activities such as summer fêtes and holiday outings were organized by the church.

Fifty years later, society had changed a great deal. People who had struggled through the hard years of the Second World War wanted to make a new life for themselves. As the nation grew wealthier again, more and more people found they could afford a whole range of leisure pursuits, and churchgoing declined. At the same time, more people from other countries were choosing to make Britain their home, and some of them brought with them different faiths.

Many people light a candle in church as a way of saying a prayer. The bright burning flame is a symbol of their hope.

Landmark events in people's lives — birth, marriage, death — prompt people to ask big questions about what life is all about. At these times, many draw near the Christian church to ask their questions and to listen to what the Christian faith has to offer that might guide them in what they think and do.

Jesus is born   500 CE   1000 CE   1500 CE   2000 CE

The red bar shows when the events on this spread took place.

Christians are one of a number of faith communities in Britain today.

Throughout the ages, Christians with a sincere faith have continued to provide hope and comfort to those in need. The story of Jesus is one that still fascinates, and still inspires people to change the way they live. The story that began two thousand years ago is one that will continue.

Give to Christian Aid this Christmas

Christian Aid
We believe in life before death

In 1945 an organization was set up in Britain called Inter-Church Aid and Refugee Service. Its aim was to help families and refugees whose lives had been wrecked by the Second World War. This charity later became known as Christian Aid. Today Christian Aid works in partnership with local people to reduce poverty in over sixty countries worldwide.

The Samaritans

In 1953 a vicar named Chad Varah realized that many people suffered dreadfully from feeling alone and unable to cope. He set up a telephone line with volunteers who were trained to listen sympathetically and help the people who called to find ways out of their bleak situation. This service, known as the Samaritans (after Jesus' story of the Good Samaritan), is offered in every community and helps many thousands of people each year.

C.S. Lewis

The famous children's stories by C.S. Lewis (1898–1963) explore many Christian ideas. In the imaginary land of Narnia, children meet the mysterious and wise lion Aslan. Like Jesus, he invites children to undertake great adventures in which they face the challenge of choosing between good and evil.

The story of Jesus' birth is, for Christians, the story of God coming to earth as a person to bring love and joy. Each year, at Christmas, the story is retold time and again, and both enchants and inspires many who do not consider themselves to have a religious faith.

During the Second World War, Coventry cathedral was destroyed. After the war, a new cathedral was built and became a centre for reconciliation or restoring good relations between people. The cathedral worked to restore relations with the people of Dresden, a German town badly bombed by the British in the war. At one end of the old cathedral remains, pictured here, are the simple Altar of Reconciliation, made from fragments of stone, and the Charred Cross, constructed from beams burnt during the bombing in November 1940.

Did you know?

By the 1990s only around ten per cent of the British population said that they were regular churchgoers.

Index